FLAVOURS SERIES

Blueberries

Elaine Elliot and Virginia Lee

Formac Publishing Company Limited
Halifax, Nova Scotia .

Authors' note

In continuing the theme of the **Flavours** *series of cookbooks, we have invited chefs from across Canada to share their recipes, and we thank them for their generosity. Each recipe has been tested and adjusted for the home cook.*

— *Elaine Elliot and Virginia Lee*

Participating restaurants

British Columbia
All Seasons Café, Nelson
Kingfisher Resort and Spa, Royston
Old House Restaurant, Courtenay
RainCoast Café, Tofino

Alberta
Lake Louise Station, Lake Louise

Saskatchewan
Boffins Club, Saskatoon

Ontario
Edgewater Manor Restaurant, Stoney Creek
Envers Restaurant, Morriston
Little Inn of Bayfield, Bayfield
Solé Restaurant and Wine Bar, Waterloo
Vineland Estates Winery Restaurant, Vineland

Québec
L'Astral at Loews Le Concorde Hotel, Quebéc City

New Brunswick
Dufferin Inn and San Martello Dining Room, Saint John
Inn on the Cove and Spa, Saint John
Marshlands Inn, Sackville
Quaco Inn, St. Martins

Prince Edward Island
Dalvay by the Sea, Dalvay
The Dunes Café, Brackley Beach
The Inn at Bay Fortune, Bay Fortune

Nova Scotia
Acton's Grill and Café, Wolfville
Amherst Shore Country Inn, Lorneville
Blomidon Inn, Wolfville
Bluenose Lodge, Lunenburg
Duncreigan Country Inn, Mabou
Falcourt Inn, Nictaux
Garrison House Inn, Annapolis Royal
Gowrie House Country Inn, Sydney Mines
Haddon Hall Inn, Chester
Inn on the Lake, Fall River
Keltic Lodge, Ingonish
La Perla, Dartmouth
Mountain Gap Inn, Smiths Cove
Pines Resort, Digby

Formac Publishing Company Limited acknowledges the support of the Culture Division, Nova Scotia Department of Tourism, Culture and Heritage. We acknowledge the financial support of the Government of Canada through the Book Publishing Industry Development Program (BPIDP) for our publishing activities.
We acknowledge the support of the Canada Council for the Arts for our publishing program.

Library and Archives Canada Cataloguing in Publication
Elliot, Elaine, 1939-
      Blueberries : recipes from Canada's best chefs / Elaine
Elliot & Virginia Lee.
(Flavours series)
ISBN 10: 0-88780-681-3, ISBN 13: 978-0-88780-681-0
      1. Cookery (Blueberries) 2. Cookery, Canadian.
I. Lee, Virginia, 1947- II. Title. III. Series.
TX813.B5E44 2005   641.6'4737   C2005-903638-9

Formac Publishing Company Limited
5502 Atlantic Street
Halifax, Nova Scotia B3H 1G4
www.formac.ca

Printed and bound in China

Contents

Introduction

It's hard to say how long we've been putting fresh and frozen blueberries in muffins, pies, cobblers, grunts and smoothies and on top of our cereal. Before North Americans started cultivating them, they had been growing in the wild for centuries. The best news in recent years is that they not only taste great, but they're also good for us. In fact, researchers have found that, among all fruits and vegetables, these small round berries contain the highest amount of important disease-fighting antioxidants.

They might be small, but blueberries pack a big punch—both for our health and our economy. Every year in Canada, hailing from farms as widespread as those in British Columbia's Fraser Valley to ones in Oxford, Nova Scotia, blueberry crops generate almost $100 million. To give you an idea of the size of the industry, 18.5 million kilograms of wild blueberries were produced in Nova Scotia in 2004, while Quebec harvested 20 million kilograms.

Sometimes tart or sweet, blueberries are members of the family *Ericaceae*, which includes heath plants, heathers, azaleas and rhododendrons

and, more specifically, the genus *Vaccinium*. About 450 wild species of the deciduous *Ericaceae* family may be found in areas throughout the Northern Hemisphere, Asia and parts of South America. Of these, 18 occur in Canada, all of which are shrubs whose berries range in colour from blue to red to black.

The blueberry shares its generic designation with many other edible berry-producing plants whose names reflect the distinctiveness of their area of origin: lingonberry, whortleberry, partridgeberry, huckleberry, sparkleberry and cranberry. In England, the fruit is known as the bilberry; in western parts of that country, the same fruit historically was known as either whortleberry or hurtleberry for the colour of its skin, which reminded some of "hurted" or bruised human flesh. In America, these two names joined to form "huckleberry," a close cousin of the blueberry and a name that seemed to typify the hardy, intrepid spirit of the American people immortalized in Mark Twain's *The Adventures of Huckleberry Finn*. Though blueberries and huckleberries are often confused, they are not the same plant; huckleberries have a darker skin and more prominent seeds than their smaller relative.

Upon their arrival in the New World, European explorers found that the Aboriginal peoples prized blueberries as a source both of food and medicine, gathering them in abundance during the summer months in woodlands and bogs and on rocky hillsides and eating them fresh or dried. The natives generously shared with settlers the recipe for blueberry root tea, a muscle relaxant to ease the pain of childbirth. Other parts of the blueberry plant were used to treat various stomach ailments and chest infections.

In 1615, Samuel de Champlain watched the Aboriginals gather and dry blueberries in the Lake Huron region. Once dried, blueberries were crushed and mixed with cornmeal, water and honey to make a pudding called "sautauthig." On their momentous overland voyage to the edge of the Pacific Ocean, which took place from 1804-06, explorers Meriwether Lewis and William Clark observed Native Americans adding crushed blueberries to their meat before curing it. This step ensured a vital supply of vitamins during the long winter months, when scurvy was rampant.

In his 1672 book, *New England's Rarities*, English traveller John Josselyn extolled the "sky-coloured billberries" he encountered in the New World that were much bluer than the whortleberries of his native country. He wrote that "the Indians dry them in the sun and sell them to the English by the Bushell." English colonists happily substituted these dried berries for currants in their traditional dessert recipes; during blueberry season, they created a new delicacy from the fresh fruit, a "summer pudding" made from the berries and sweetened, spiced milk or sherry.

Although we may feel that these delicious berries are a gift directly from nature to us, human consumption is only a small part of their story. Heath plants also are an important food source for wildlife. Birds, small animals such as rabbits, foxes

and rodents and larger animals such as deer, caribou and bears eat the berries, twigs and leaves of the blueberry plant. It has been said that bears can smell the berries as they ripen and will travel miles to search out their scent.

The blueberry is one of the rare fruits to be marketed in both its wild and cultivated forms. Lowbush wild blueberries (*Vaccinium angustifolium*), descriptively called "star berries" because of the star-shaped calyx on the top, reach a height of 0.3 to 0.6 metres, or one to two feet, and are extremely hardy. This variety spreads by underground rhizomes, creating widespread colonies commonly called "blueberry barrens."

Northern highbush (*Vacinnium corymbosum*) can be found in the wild in wetlands and upland wooded slopes and will grow from about two to three-and-a-half metres high. Rabbiteye blueberries, or *Vacinnium ashei*, named because the calyx resembles the eye of a rabbit, flourish in the mild winter regions of the southern United States. About 100 years ago, American botanist Frederick Colville began experimenting with the hybridization of different wild highbush varieties in his native New Jersey. Among these early ones were the predictably named Earliblue, Late Blue, Blueray and Bluetta. Colville's success at cultivating large, flavourful berries led to the birth of a new industry.

Over the decades, plant breeders have fine-tuned commercially grown blueberries, developing early, mid-season and late-producing hybrids to suit both the fresh and frozen food-processing markets. Long-lived and thriving in acidic soil, blueberries have become a lucrative crop in areas where traditional agriculture doesn't flourish.

The leading producer of blueberries in the world is North America, its market share accounting for an impressive 85 per cent of global production. Cultivated highbush harvesting begins in the spring in the southern United States and continues in Nova Scotia and British Columbia into October. The ideal growing conditions in the Lower Fraser Valley make British Columbia the second-largest cultivated blueberry producer in the world. Highbush berries are grown in British Columbia and on a much smaller scale in Ontario, Quebec and the Maritimes.

Wild lowbush blueberries are harvested in midsummer throughout Atlantic Canada, Quebec and Maine, with an average annual production of about 900 tonnes. Canada is the top wild blueberry producer in the world, while Nova Scotia contributes one-quarter of the total amount. The industry in that province started to take shape in the 1930s and 1940s, when entire families travelled to the Cumberland County barrens to harvest blueberries in late summer. They would set up camp for several weeks to hand pick the fruit, which was used as a winter food source, as well as a cash crop. As markets grew, producers would hire workers to harvest the berries (by this time, the manual rake was being used).

The first modern-world standard freezing-and-processing facility was built in Springhill, Nova Scotia, in 1962. The development of the "individual quick-freezing technology" meant that blueberries could be frozen—preserving their

colour, taste and texture for up to two years—and used in other products, as well as being available year-round, making them even more marketable.

In 1968, Cumberland County was the setting for a small company called Oxford Frozen Foods, which had plans to put the wild blueberry on the world stage; today it's the world's largest processor of wild blueberries. In 1984, the Bragg Lumber Company in the same county produced the first commercially successful mechanical blueberry harvester in North America, which replaced the manual rake and cut harvesting costs by up to 50 per cent.

Blueberries have been good to the East Coast, and vice versa. Hardy lowbush blueberries thrive in the acidic soil with very little help from humans; to maximize plant and berry growth, producers allow blueberry fields to lie fallow every other year. Over-burning and the cutting back of shrubs also are done in fallow years, a reflection of nature's lightning strikes and brush fires that, paradoxically, stimulate the growth of branches and flowers the following year.

Unlike many other soft fruit, blueberries can be grown successfully with few pesticides and chemical fertilizers. So-called wild blueberries sold in grocery stores have likely been sprayed to protect the crop from infestation and fungus. Only berries grown and picked in the wild or from a certified organic grower may be deemed both wild and organic. Though many Maritimers will recall the backbreaking labour of hand raking lowbush blueberries as a summer job, modern mechanical pickers now harvest most of the crop. However, the uneven terrain on which many wild blueberries grow ensures that the traditional hand-raking practice is far from obsolete. To reduce bruising, highbush producers prefer old-fashioned hand picking.

Blueberries are brought to one of two markets, fresh or processed, each accounting for 50 per cent of total sales. In the world of perishable fresh fruit, time is of the essence; newly picked berries are rushed to packinghouses and airports for immediate distribution to both local and international markets.

Throughout history, certain foods have been celebrated in folk medicine as having curative and preventive medical properties. Today health researchers are attempting to validate the scientific value of these foods. It appears that Mother Nature has bestowed a great deal of health-promoting ingredients on the North American blueberry, and scientists are discovering that they are very good for us.

Like many vibrantly coloured fruits and vegetables, blueberries have high nutritional value, are rich in fibre and contain Vitamin C. Anthocyanin, the pigment that produces blueberries' striking blue colour, makes them high in antioxidant activity. In test-tube studies, antioxidants help fight cancer and reduce inflammation, which occurs in diseases such as arthritis and inflammatory bowel disease. Antioxidants are more concentrated in the smaller wild berries, which also have a higher fibre content.

Positive results from animal studies show that blueberries may prevent age-related loss of mental

capacity and improve short-term memory and motor co-ordination. These cancer and heart disease fighters subdue the harmful "free radicals" produced by our bodies. Like cranberries, blueberries may act as an antibacterial agent to reduce the incidence and severity of urinary tract infections. In Japan, the wild blueberry is nicknamed "vision fruit," since it reportedly improves night vision and reduces eye fatigue.

One half-cup (125 ml) serving of fresh or unsweetened frozen blueberries has 40 calories and is a valuable source of manganese, potassium and Vitamins A, C and K. Blueberries are low in sodium, have only trace amounts of fat, provide folic acid and offer a good supply of dietary fibre.

Unlike some seasonal fruits, blueberries are preserved in various ways so we can buy them year-round. Traditional jams and jellies, frozen berries and canned pie filling have been joined on grocery-store shelves by new products such as blueberry juice and dried blueberries. Now flash-frozen at very low temperatures to cut down on clumping, the frozen fruit will keep for up to two years and can be substituted for fresh berries when baking.

A great snack or cereal topping, dried blueberries are made with fresh or frozen fruit infused with a sugar solution to keep the dried berry soft, then dehydrated with hot air, reducing their moisture content to around 20 per cent. Berries can be dried at home by placing a cookie sheet with a layer of berries in a sunny place for four or five days, or by baking in a very low (150°F) oven for four to five hours. Completely dry berries will keep indefinitely in a plastic bag or glass jar.

A new appreciation for the foods we eat and the people who produce them has been generated by the global Slow Food Movement, as a growing number of dedicated chefs and consumers are putting into practice their philosophy of food selection. Originating in Italy in 1986, this movement now boasts more than 80,000 members worldwide.

For "slow fooders," the change begins with choosing locally grown foods whenever possible, which helps farmers and the environment by cutting down on the air pollution generated by fleets of food transport trucks criss-crossing North America. Blueberries are an ideal and easily accessible slow-food delicacy that often grow in our own backyards.

Canadian chefs dedicated to this culinary concept have contributed several recipes to this revised edition of *Blueberries*. Within these pages you'll discover how to make such decadent desserts as Fresh Blueberry and White Chocolate Victoria and Blueberry, Mango and Hazelnut Cobbler—a twist on the traditional—plus some delightful blueberry appetizers and entrées, such as Blueberry and Goat Cheese Soufflé. This book will give readers an appreciation both for the people who work in the blueberry industry and the culinary professionals who creatively incorporate this native North American fruit into all kinds of dishes, from the first to the last course and everything in between.

Blueberry Conserve, p.27

Breakfast Dishes

We can't think of a better way to start the day than to sit down to a bowl of fresh blueberries. Or perhaps you would like to try Blueberry Cinnamon Coffee Cake. For that special weekend breakfast, be sure to try Buttermilk Blueberry Pancakes topped with pure maple syrup!

Blueberry Cinnamon Coffee Cake

Inn on the Lake, Fall River, NS

Blueberry season is a special time at the Inn on the Lake, as the chefs adapt a variety of different recipes to include blueberries.

1 cup (250 mL) fresh blueberries
1 tsp (5 mL) cinnamon
½ cup (125 mL) butter
1 cup (250 mL) granulated sugar
2 eggs
1½ tsp (7 mL) vanilla
1½ cups (375 mL) all-purpose flour
2 tsp (10 mL) baking powder
¼ tsp (1 mL) salt
⅔ cup (150 mL) milk
blueberry sauce (recipe follows)
whipped cream, as garnish (optional)

Preheat oven to 350°F (180°C). Toss blueberries with cinnamon and set aside. Cream butter and sugar together until fluffy. Beat in eggs, one at a time; add vanilla. Sift together flour, baking powder and salt. Add flour to butter mixture, alternately with milk, in three additions. Fold in blueberries. Pour batter into a greased 10-inch (23-cm) round springform pan and bake for 40-45 minutes. Cake is ready when a toothpick inserted in the centre comes out clean. Let cool for 20 minutes, unmold and serve with warm blueberry sauce and whipped cream.

Serves 10-12.

Blueberry Sauce
1 cup (250 mL) blueberries
1 cup (250 mL) granulated sugar
1 tbsp (15 mL) cornstarch, mixed in
¼ cup (60 mL) cold water

Combine all ingredients in a saucepan, bring to a boil and cook until thickened. Serve warm over coffee cake.

Blueberry Lassi

Chilled yoghurt-based drinks are popular in India and other tropical countries. We like to think of them as a healthy alternative to the milkshake. For a thinner-style lassi you may substitute buttermilk or whole milk for the yoghurt.

2 cups (500 mL) blueberries
1 cup (250 mL) blueberry juice (optional orange or pineapple juice)
2 cups (500 mL) plain yoghurt
2 tbsp (30 mL) superfine sugar
ice cubes
mint leaves, as garnish

Combine the blueberries, blueberry juice, yoghurt and sugar in a blender and purée until smooth. Pass the liquid through a fine-mesh sieve to remove seeds and skins. To serve, place ice cubes in a tall glass, add the lassi and garnish with a mint leaf.

Yields 4 servings.

Blueberry Scones

Buttery, warm and slightly sweet, these easy-to-prepare breakfast treats are guaranteed to start your day on a happy note.

2¼ cups (550 mL) all-purpose flour
½ cup (125 mL) granulated sugar
4 tsp (20 mL) baking powder
½ cup (125 mL) butter
¾ cup (175 mL) dried blueberries
⅔ cup (150 mL) buttermilk
2 eggs

In a large bowl, combine flour, sugar and baking powder. Cut in butter until mixture resembles coarse crumbs. Add blueberries to dry mixture, stirring to combine.

In a small bowl, whisk together buttermilk and eggs. Add buttermilk mixture to dry mixture stirring with a fork until just combined. Spoon batter into 12 individual portions on a parchment paper-lined baking sheet. Bake in preheated 375°F (190°C) oven until cooked and lightly browned on top, about 15-18 minutes. Serve warm or cold.

Yields 1 dozen scones.

Blueberry Lemon Muffins

If you want to keep some of these muffins for breakfast, you would be well advised to hide them. They are simply the best blueberry muffins we have ever tasted.

2 cups (500 mL) all-purpose flour
½ cup (125 mL) granulated sugar
½ tsp (2 mL) salt
1 tbsp (15 mL) baking powder
1 egg, beaten
zest of 1 lemon
1 cup (250 mL) milk
½ cup (125 mL) butter, melted
1¼ cup (300 mL) fresh or frozen blueberries
¼ cup (60 mL) butter, melted (2nd amount)
1 tbsp (15 mL) lemon juice
¼ cup (60 mL) granulated sugar (2nd amount)

Preheat oven to 400°F (200°C). Sift flour, sugar, salt and baking powder into a large bowl. Whisk beaten egg, lemon zest, milk and melted butter, and stir into dry ingredients until just blended. Stir in blueberries. Fill prepared muffin tins two-thirds full and bake for 20 minutes.

While muffins are baking, combine melted butter and lemon juice in a small bowl. Measure sugar in a separate bowl. When muffins are slightly cooled, dip tops first in lemon butter and then in sugar.

Yields 18 muffins.

Baked Blueberry French Toast

Smart hosts and late-rising weekend cooks alike will enjoy whipping up this short-order breakfast/brunch that begins the night before.

1 loaf French bread or baguette (15-20 slices)
6 eggs
1 cup (250 mL) milk
pinch of baking powder
¼ tsp (1 mL) ground nutmeg
1 tsp (5 mL) vanilla extract
5 cups (1.25 L) blueberries
½ cup (125 mL) granulated sugar
1 tsp (5 mL) ground cinnamon
1-2 tsp (5-10 mL) cornstarch (larger quantity if
   using frozen berries)
2 tbsp (30 mL) melted butter
icing sugar

Slice the bread diagonally in ¾-inch (2-cm) slices and discard the ends. Place the bread in a single layer in a large baking dish or on a rimmed baking sheet. In a bowl, whisk together eggs, milk, baking powder, nutmeg and vanilla. Pour the egg mixture over the bread; turn the slices to absorb the liquid. Cover the bread with plastic wrap and refrigerate overnight.

Preheat oven to 400°F (200°C). In a bowl, toss blueberries with sugar, cinnamon and cornstarch. Butter a large baking dish and cover bottom with blueberry mixture. Arrange bread slices over blueberries (you may have to cut some slices to fit). Brush bread with melted butter and bake for 30-40 minutes until the berries bubble around the edges and the toast is golden. Remove from oven and let sit for a few minutes.

To serve, arrange the slices on plates, spoon blueberry sauce over them and dust with icing sugar.

Serves 6.

Gingered Fruit Compote

Tart fresh lime tempers the sweetness of this variation on fruit salad. Great as a topping for vanilla yoghurt or ice cream, it serves double duty at breakfast and dessert time and is flexible when it comes to ingredients.

2 cups (500 mL) blueberries
2 cups (500 mL) fresh pineapple, cubed
1 large orange, segmented and with the white
   pith removed
1 tbsp (15 mL) diced crystallized ginger
1½ tbsp (22 mL) liquid honey
1 tbsp (15 mL) lime juice
zest of 1 lime

Add fruit and ginger to a serving bowl. In a small bowl, blend honey, lime juice and zest; pour over fruit and stir to combine. Serve chilled or at room temperature.

Yields 5 cups.

Blueberry Waffles

Crispy nut-brown waffles are a nice variation from pancakes at Sunday brunch. Treat yourself and cover them with butter and your favourite syrup.

1½ cups (375 mL) all-purpose flour
2 tbsp (30 mL) granulated sugar
½ tsp (2 mL) salt
½ tsp (2 mL) baking soda
1 tsp (5 mL) baking powder
1½ cups (375 mL) buttermilk
2 eggs, beaten
¼ cup (50 mL) vegetable oil or melted butter
½ cup (125 mL) blueberries, washed and dried

Combine flour, sugar, salt, baking soda and baking powder in a large bowl. In another bowl, whisk together buttermilk, eggs and oil. Add liquid to dry ingredients, stirring only until smooth.

Preheat waffle iron according to manufacturer's directions. Pour batter onto hot waffle iron and sprinkle with 1 tbsp (15 mL) blueberries. Bake until steaming stops and waffle is golden. Serve immediately.

Serves 4.

Buttermilk Blueberry Pancakes

We have been making these pancakes for so long that the recipe is firmly imprinted in our memory. Once you try them they will become the pancake of choice for your family as well!

1½ cups (375 mL) all-purpose flour
1 tsp (5 mL) baking powder
½ tsp (2 mL) salt
½ tsp (2 mL) baking soda
2 tbsp (30 mL) granulated sugar
1¾ cups (425 mL) buttermilk
2 tbsp (30 mL) vegetable oil
1 egg
½ cup (125 mL) blueberries, fresh or frozen

Sift flour, baking powder, salt, baking soda and sugar into a large bowl. In another bowl, beat together buttermilk, vegetable oil and egg. Add liquid to flour mixture, stirring only until combined. Drop by large spoonful onto a greased hot griddle and sprinkle with blueberries. Cook until pancake bubbles; turn and cook on other side until golden brown. Serve hot with syrup of choice.

Yields 10-12 medium pancakes.

Blueberry Melon Smoothie

Boffins Club, Saskatoon, SK

Smooth frazzled morning nerves with this delicious yoghurt-based shake.

2 cups (500 mL) cubed honeydew melon
½ cup (125 mL) blueberries
1 cup (250 mL) plain low-fat yoghurt
1 tbsp (15 mL) light brown sugar
⅛ tsp (0.5 mL) ground cloves
1 tbsp (15 mL) liquid honey
mint leaves, as garnish

Combine all ingredients in a food processor or blender and mix 1 minute or until smooth. Pour into glasses and garnish with a sprig of mint. Serve immediately.

Yields 2 cups (500 mL).

Quick & Easy Granola Bars

Easy and economical, these tasty granola bars are ideal for times when you are unable to enjoy a sit-down breakfast. A healthy and child-appealing alternative to after-school cookies.

1½ cups (375 mL) quick oats
1 cup (250 mL) dried blueberries
¾ cup (175 mL) slivered almonds
¼ cup (60 mL) brown sugar
1 tsp (5 mL) ground cinnamon
½ cup (125 mL) liquid honey
3 tbsp (45 mL) vegetable oil

In a large bowl, combine oats, blueberries, almonds, sugar and cinnamon and stir to combine. Mix together honey and oil; add to oat mixture and stir to combine. Spread and press mixture gently in a greased 9 x 9-inch (23 x 23-cm) baking pan. Bake in preheated 350°F (180°C) oven until bars are lightly browned, about 25-30 minutes. Cool in pan on a wire rack before cutting.

Makes 18 bars.

Blueberry Conserve

A bottle of homemade jam makes a wonderful hostess gift, so be sure to make several bottles to share with friends. This conserve is delicious on muffins or toast.

6 cups (1.5 L) wild blueberries
3 cups (750 mL) granulated sugar
4 tbsp (60 mL) lemon juice

Rinse and pick over blueberries, discarding small stems or leaves. Crush berries and place them in a large preserving kettle. Stir in sugar and lemon juice. Over low heat, stir until sugar is dissolved, then bring mixture to a full rolling boil. Cook uncovered for 10-12 minutes, stirring frequently. Remove kettle from heat and let it stand for 5 minutes, skimming off any foam with a large metal spoon. Pour conserve into hot sterilized jars and seal. Refrigerate for immediate use or process for 15-20 minutes in a boiling-water canner for long-term preserving.

Yields 4 cups (1 L).

Assorted Greens with Blueberry Vinaigrette, p.30

Starters and Accompaniments

Blueberries are more than just dessert. Canadian chefs

have found ways to make them a versatile ingredient.

Be sure to try Iced Blueberry Soup or Blueberry

Vinaigrette served on assorted greens.

Assorted Greens with Blueberry Vinaigrette

Amherst Shore Country Inn, Lorneville, NS

This salad has great eye appeal because of its unique colours. If fresh blueberries are not available for the salad, the chef suggests using chopped celery or halved green or red seedless grapes.

10-12 cups (2.5-3 L) assorted greens: any combination of romaine, spinach, red, oak or regular green leaf lettuce
2 firm apples
1 cup (250 mL) fresh blueberries
blueberry vinaigrette (recipe follows)

Wash and dry greens; tear into medium-sized pieces. Core apples, but do not peel; slice in thin strips on top of lettuce. Sprinkle fresh blueberries on top. Drizzle with 2-3 tbsp (30-45 mL) blueberry vinaigrette.

Makes 6-8 servings.

Blueberry Vinaigrette

½ cup (125 mL) olive oil
¼ cup (50 mL) cider vinegar
⅛ tsp (0.5 mL) minced fresh garlic
½ tsp (2 mL) finely chopped green pepper
½ tsp (2 mL) finely chopped onion
1 tsp (5 mL) granulated sugar
1 cup (250 mL) fresh or frozen blueberries

Place all vinaigrette ingredients in a food processor and blend until vegetables are puréed. Strain through a sieve to remove small seeds. Refrigerate dressing until needed.

Yields about 1½ cups (375 mL).

Iced Blueberry Soup

Try this very attractive soup served ice cold on a warm summer's day.

5 cups (1.25 L) blueberries, washed and dried
⅔ cup (150 mL) water
½ cup (125 mL) dry white wine
¼ cup (60 mL) caster sugar*
¼ tsp (1 mL) allspice
grating of nutmeg
½ tsp (2 mL) fresh lemon juice
1¼ cups (300 mL) buttermilk

Prepare blueberries and set aside ¼ cup (50 mL) for garnish. Purée berries, water and wine in a food processor. Strain purée through a fine-mesh strainer into a large bowl.

Stir sugar, cinnamon, nutmeg, lemon juice and buttermilk into blueberry purée. Refrigerate 4-5 hours for flavours to blend. Serve chilled, garnished with reserved fresh blueberries.

Serves 4-6.

* If you cannot buy commercial caster (superfine) sugar, prepare your own by crushing regular granulated sugar in a food processor until very fine.

Blueberry Chutney

Chutneys are wonderful staples to have on hand at the back of your refrigerator. Use them to jazz up an ordinary meat or seafood dish or to make an impromptu appetizer. Simply pour a generous amount of this colourful blue chutney over a block of soft cheese and serve with assorted crackers.

½ cup (125 mL) brown sugar, firmly packed
¼ tsp (1 mL) cinnamon
⅛ tsp (0.5 mL) red pepper flakes
4 whole cloves
⅛ tsp (0.5 mL) nutmeg, freshly grated
½ cup (125 mL) red wine vinegar
½ cup (125 mL) orange juice
¼ cup (60 mL) crystallized ginger, finely chopped
½ cup (125 mL) dried apricots, chopped
½ cup (125 mL) raisins
2 lemons, juice and zest (thinly grated rind)
4 cups (1 L) blueberries, fresh or frozen

Combine all ingredients in a large saucepan. Bring the chutney to a boil, stirring constantly, until sugar is dissolved. Cover, reduce heat and simmer, stirring occasionally, until fruit is tender and thickened. Seal in sterilized jars.

Yields three 8-oz/250-mL jars.

Cinnamon Tortilla Chips with Mixed Fruit Salsa

Boffins Club, Saskatoon, SK

There are countless recipes for tortilla chips and salsa, but we have to admit this is the first time we have tried sugar-sweetened chips with a fresh fruit salsa. This variation on a Mexican classic is sure to please family and guests. Feel free to vary the salsa using any fresh seasonal fruit.

¾ cup (175 mL) fresh wild blueberries
½ cup (125 mL) raspberries
½ cup (125 mL) diced honeydew melon
½ cup (125 mL) diced cantaloupe
½ cup (125 mL) diced seedless grapes
½ cup (125 mL) diced kiwi
½ cup (125 mL) diced mango
½ cup (125 mL) diced strawberries
¼ cup (60 mL) mango purée
½ cup brown sugar (preferably organic cane sugar)
2 tbsp (30 mL) ground cinnamon
10 flour tortillas
vegetable oil, as needed

Peel, seed and stem fruit as necessary; dice by hand. In a blender, purée a small amount of mango to equal ¼ cup (60 mL). Add blueberries, raspberries, diced fruit, and mango purée to a bowl and gently mix. Cover and refrigerate until ready to use.

In a large bowl, combine brown sugar and cinnamon; reserve. Cut tortillas into small triangles. In a large saucepan, pour vegetable oil to a depth of 3 inches (8 cm) and heat to 350°F (180°C). Using a basket strainer, carefully place a handful of tortillas into the hot oil and cook for 1-2 minutes or until crispy. Remove basket from saucepan, carefully shake off excess oil and immediately place chips into the sugar-cinnamon mixture. Toss chips to coat and place on serving dish. Repeat process with remaining tortilla chips.

To serve: place crisped tortilla chips in a serving bowl accompanied with fruit salsa for dipping.

Serves 6.

Blueberry and Goat Cheese Soufflés

Solé Restaurant and Wine Bar, Waterloo, ON

Served straight from the oven, these light and airy starters taste heavenly as they melt in your mouth.

1 tbsp (15 mL) cold butter
½ cup (125 mL) fine breadcrumbs
1 cup (250 mL) whole milk (3.25% M.F.)
3 cloves
½ cup (125 mL) chopped onion
pinch each of nutmeg and dry mustard
2½ tbsp (37 mL) butter (2nd amount)
⅓ cup (75 mL) all-purpose flour
¾ cup (175 mL) goat cheese (chèvre)
4 egg yolks, lightly beaten
½ tsp (2 mL) each of salt and pepper
5 (2 mL) egg whites
6 tbsp (90 mL) blueberries

Rub the inside of six 1-cup (250-mL) ramekins with cold butter and dust with bread crumbs, shaking to remove excess. Place ramekins on a baking sheet and refrigerate until ready to use.

In a saucepan, combine milk, cloves, onion, nutmeg and mustard. Bring to a boil, remove from heat and strain to remove solids. Reserve. Wipe out saucepan, add butter (2nd amount) and melt over medium heat; whisk in flour and cook one minute, stirring constantly. Whisk reserved milk mixture into saucepan, add ⅔ cup (150 mL) of the goat cheese and stir to melt. Remove from heat and whisk egg yolks into mixture until well blended. Add salt and pepper, return to heat and, stirring constantly, bring liquid just to boiling point. Remove from heat and reduce temperature of cheese mixture to warm.

At this point, preheat oven to 400°F (200°C) and place a large roaster in oven with enough hot water to allow a depth of ½ inch (1 cm) when ramekins are added. Beat egg whites with salt until stiff peaks form. Stir half of the whites into the cheese mixture and with a spatula gently fold in the remaining whites, being careful not to overmix.

Fill chilled ramekins half-way, add 1 tbsp (15 mL) blueberries and 1 tsp (5 mL) goat cheese to each ramekin and fill to the top with remaining batter. Gently smooth tops with spatula. Place ramekins in water bath and bake until soufflés are golden brown and almost double in size, about 20 minutes. Serve immediately with tossed salad of choice.

Serves 6.

Spinach Salad with Smoked Ahi Tuna and Blueberry Dressing

RainCoast Café, Tofino, BC

Chef/owner Lisa Henderson shares with us a delightful spinach salad with a distinctive Pacific Rim flavour.

baby spinach or mesclun mix to serve 6
blueberry dressing (recipe follows)
2 cups (500 mL) sugared pecans (recipe follows)
6-8 oz (180-250 g) sliced smoked Ahi tuna (or smoked salmon)
mint leaves, as garnish

Rinse and dry spinach, removing tough stems. Add spinach to a large salad bowl and toss with dressing. Divide salad among 6 large plates. Scatter sugared pecans decoratively around plate. Roll tuna into rosettes and place alongside spinach. Garnish with mint leaves.

Serves 6.

Blueberry Dressing
2 tbsp (30 mL) mirin (Japanese rice wine)
2 tbsp (30 mL) fresh lemon juice
¼ cup (60 mL) olive oil
⅓ cup (75 mL) blueberries
⅓ cup (75 mL) sour cream
1 tbsp (15 mL) granulated sugar
pinch of ground star anise

In a blender, combine all ingredients and blend until smooth and creamy.

Makes ¾ cup (175 mL).

Sugared Pecans
1 egg white
½ tsp (2 mL) water
2 cups (500 mL) pecans
¼ cup (50 mL) granulated sugar
¾ tsp (3 mL) cinnamon

In a bowl, whisk egg white and water until frothy; stir in pecans. Combine sugar and cinnamon and stir into pecan mixture. Spread nuts in a single layer on parchment paper-lined baking sheet and bake in preheated 250ºF (121ºC) oven until dry, about 45 minutes. Cool, break up and store in refrigerator.

Makes 2 cups (500 mL).

Pecan Crostini with Brie and Blueberries

Old House Restaurant, Courtenay, BC

We like appetizers that are simple to prepare. This easy hors d'oeuvre also gets the nod for flavour and eye appeal.

1 whole wheat baguette
1 wheel of Brie (8 oz/ 250 g)
¼ cup (60 mL) blueberries
pinch of Cajun spice
30 large pecan halves

Slice baguette into ¼-inch (0.5-cm) slices and set aside. Cover with a tea towel to keep fresh. Slice Brie into enough small wedges to place one on each baguette slice. Crush blueberries together with Cajun spice. Spread on bread slices. Place a wedge of cheese onto each slice and top with a pecan half. Bake in a preheated 350°F (180°C) oven until warm and cheese begins to melt, about 7 minutes.

Yields about 30 pieces.

Roast Loin of Pork with Blueberry and Juniper Sauce, p.44

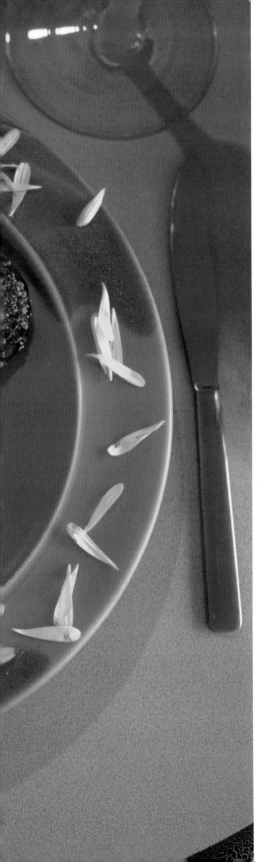

Main Dishes

Always anxious to use local ingredients, Canadian chefs
have developed wonderful recipes incorporating the
native blueberry. They have found that this flavourful
berry enhances a myriad of main course dishes.

Amherst Shore Chicken with Blueberry Sauce

Amherst Shore Country Inn, Lorneville, NS

Nova Scotia's Cumberland County blueberries are at their peak during August, and Donna Laceby uses them innovatively in several recipes. We are sure this will be one of your favourites.

4 boneless chicken breasts (5 oz/150 g)
2 tbsp (30 mL) cornstarch
3 tbsp (45 mL) water
2 cups (500 mL) fresh or frozen blueberries
3 tbsp (45 mL) granulated sugar
½ cup (125 mL) dry red wine
zest of 1 lemon

Preheat oven to 375°F (190°C). Rinse and pat dry chicken breasts. Over medium-high heat, grill breasts until browned, turning once. Remove to oven and bake for 5-7 minutes, or until chicken is no longer pink in the centre.

Dissolve cornstarch in water and combine with blueberries and sugar in a saucepan. Cook over medium-high heat until berries break down and sauce thickens. Add wine and bring back to a boil. To serve, spread a small amount of blueberry sauce on each plate, top with chicken breast and drizzle with remaining sauce. Sprinkle with lemon zest to garnish.

Serves 4.

Roast Duck Marshlands

Marshlands Inn, Sackville, NB

This rendition of roast duck is an easily prepared, elegant meal with a distinctively Maritime flavour. The blueberries can be stewed in advance and incorporated into the sauce at serving time.

1 duck (4½-5 lb/2-2.3 kg)
salt
2 small apples, halved
2 small onions, halved
2 cups (500 mL) fresh blueberries
2 tbsp (30 mL) water
½ cup (125 mL) granulated sugar
¼ cup (60 mL) vinegar
½ cup (125 mL) red wine
salt and pepper to taste

Preheat oven to 450°F (230°C). Rinse and pat dry duck. Season with salt and stuff with apple and onion pieces. Tie legs together with butcher's twine so duck will keep its shape while baking. Prick all over to release fat during cooking and place on a rack in a roasting pan. Place duck in oven and immediately reduce temperature to 350°F (180°C). Cook until tender and juices from the thickest part of the thigh run clear, about 20 minutes per pound (45 minutes per kilogram). Remove to a platter and tent with foil.

While duck is roasting, stew blueberries with water and sugar. Set aside. Drain fat from roasting pan, being careful to conserve the brown drippings. Put pan over high heat and deglaze with vinegar; add wine and continue scraping brown bits from pan. Reduce by half and add stewed blueberries; season with salt and pepper and simmer 5 minutes longer to further reduce sauce. Serve carved duck napped with sauce.

Serves 2-3.

Roast Loin of Pork with Blueberry and Juniper Sauce

The Dunes Café, Brackley Beach, PEI

The chef at the Dunes Café serves roast loin of pork napped with a blueberry demi-glace sauce. To aid the home cook, we are offering instructions using a commercial demi-glace mix.

3-4 lb (1.5-2 kg) pork loin, deboned and tied
1 package demi-glace (available in most grocery stores)
1¼ cups (300 mL) cold water
¼ cup (60 mL) red wine vinegar
¼ cup (60 mL) red wine
¾ cup (175 mL) blueberries, portioned
8 juniper berries (or 1 oz/30 mL gin)
1 large sprig fresh thyme
6 black peppercorns
1 small bay leaf
salt and pepper to taste

Remove pork loin from refrigerator and allow to come to room temperature. Roast in a preheated 160°F (71°C) oven, allowing 30 minutes per pound (1 hour per kilogram) or until a meat thermometer registers 160°F (71°C) when inserted into the thickest part of the roast. Remove from oven and tent with foil.

While meat is roasting, stir contents of demi-glace package into cold water and bring to a boil over medium-high heat. Reduce heat and cook until thickened. Reserve. In a separate pot combine red wine vinegar, red wine, ¼ cup (60 mL) blueberries, juniper berries, thyme, peppercorns and bay leaf. Boil until liquid is reduced by two-thirds. Strain into reserved demi-glace and stir in second amount of blueberries. Return to heat, bring to serving temperature and season with salt and pepper. Serve with slices of roasted pork loin.

Serves 6.

Peppered Loin of Caribou with Blueberry Cabernet Sauce

Envers Restaurant, Morriston, ON

Farm-raised game meats such as elk, venison, wild boar and buffalo are becoming increasingly popular in restaurants, offering diners flavourful entrée variations on the traditional beef and pork. This recipe features Canadian caribou, a very lean meat with a subtle "hint of the wild" flavour. Other venison or beef may be used in lieu of caribou.

The chef says caribou steaks are best served rare or medium-rare because they are so lean.

2 cups (500 mL) Cabernet Sauvignon wine
1 tbsp (15 mL) granulated sugar
1½ tbsp (20 mL) chopped shallot
1 garlic clove, minced
1 sprig fresh thyme
½ cup (125 ml) blueberries
3 tbsp (45 mL) chilled butter, cut in small cubes
½ cup (125 mL) dried blueberries*
salt
1½ tsp blueberry vinegar (or 7 mL red wine
    vinegar)
⅓-½ cup (75-125 mL) mixed pink, black and
    white peppercorns
2 lb (1 kg) striploin caribou steaks, cut in 8-oz
    (250-g) portions
salt (2nd amount)
3 tbsp (45 mL) vegetable oil

In a medium saucepan, add wine, sugar, shallot, garlic, thyme and blueberries. Cook over medium-high heat for 15-20 minutes or until the wine is reduced by three-quarters. Strain into a small saucepan, pressing on the solids to extract all flavour; discard solids. Bring sauce to just below the simmering point and whisk in butter, one cube at a time. Add dried blueberries and adjust seasoning with salt, vinegar and additional sugar, if necessary. Keep warm, but do not allow sauce to simmer.

Crush peppercorns until they are cracked. Season the steaks with salt and then press sides into the cracked peppercorns. Heat a cast-iron skillet to hot; add oil and quickly add steaks. Allow to cook for 3 minutes on each side for rare or until desired doneness. Remove and serve immediately.

To serve: place steaks on warmed plates and top with the warm blueberry-wine sauce. Serve with vegetables of choice.

Serves 4.

*To dry your own blueberries: arrange berries on a paper-towel-lined baking tray and bake in 220°F (100°C) oven for 4 hours with the door slightly ajar. Cool and store.

Mushroom-Crusted Chicken Stuffed with Sun-Dried Blueberry Cream

Kingfisher Resort and Spa, Royston, BC

At Kingfisher, chef Ronald St. Pierre presents this dish using "frenched" breasts of chicken. This cut features half of a skinless, boneless chicken breast with the first wing bone attached. The tip of the wing bone is removed, yielding a neat and attractive portion that lends itself to creative plate presentation. For the ease of the home chef, we have tested the recipe with boneless chicken breasts.

1 oz (30 g) dried morel mushrooms
⅓ cup (75 mL) sun-dried blueberries
1 cup (250 mL) warm water
4 oz (125 g) cream cheese
2 tbsp (30 mL) finely chopped fresh parsley
2 tsp (10 mL) lemon zest
1½ tsp (8 mL) Dijon mustard
¼ tsp (1 mL) coarsely ground black pepper
salt
mushroom duxelle (recipe follows)
6 skinless, boneless chicken breasts (4 oz/125 g
    each)
1-2 tbsp (15-30 mL) vegetable oil
3 tbsp (45 mL) finely chopped shallots
¼ cup (60 mL) dry red wine
3 tbsp (45 mL) rose petal vinegar (or white wine
    vinegar)
⅓ cup (75 mL) blueberry conserve (see page 27)

salt and pepper
fresh chopped chives, as garnish

In a food processor, add morel mushrooms and pulse until crumblike. Remove to a plate and reserve.

In a bowl, soak blueberries in warm water for 10 minutes to soften. Drain the blueberries and reserve the water for the sauce. In a small bowl, combine cream cheese, parsley, lemon zest, mustard and pepper until blended. Adjust seasoning with salt to taste; reserve.

Prepare chicken by slicing in the side of each breast, being careful not to cut all the way through. Open the breast and gently flatten the

meat. Portion equal amounts of mushroom duxelle on each breast, being careful not to extend it to the edges. Top with cream cheese mixture. Close breasts, tucking edges in to form a neat package. Coat the chicken with the reserved morel mushroom mixture, pressing to adhere. If preparing in advance, you can place breasts on a baking sheet, cover with plastic wrap and refrigerate until ready to cook.

Heat oil in a large skillet over medium-high heat; add breasts, being careful not to crowd. Cook on both sides until lightly coloured. Remove breasts to an ovenproof dish and bake in 350°F (180°C) oven for 10 minutes or until cooked.

Meanwhile, remove excess oil from skillet and sauté shallots until tender. Raise heat to medium-high and deglaze with red wine; add vinegar and reserved blueberry water; reduce by three-quarters. Add blueberry conserve and season with salt and pepper to taste.

To serve: arrange chicken on serving plates with vegetables of choice; nap chicken with blueberry sauce and garnish with fresh chopped chives.

Serves 6.

Mushroom Duxelle
1 tsp (5 mL) olive oil
2 tbsp (30 mL) minced shallots
1 garlic clove, minced
6 oz (200 g) white mushrooms, finely chopped
1 tsp (5 mL) chopped fresh thyme
1 tbsp (15 mL) brandy
salt and pepper
1 tbsp (15 mL) chopped fresh parsley

Add olive oil to a skillet over medium heat; add shallots and garlic and sauté until tender. Reduce heat to medium-low, add mushrooms and thyme and continue cooking, stirring frequently, until dry. Deglaze with brandy and flambé. Season with salt and pepper, and stir in parsley. Cool and reserve.

Yields about ¾ cup (175 mL).

Pork Tenderloin Medallions with Blueberries and Cheese

Lake Louise Station, Lake Louise, AB

Chef Hung Khuu at Lake Louise Station specializes in innovative Albertan fare. This succulent pork entrée served on a rosemary-infused jus is destined for fame among hosts since it can be prepared up to the point of baking prior to the arrival of guests.

½ cup (125 mL) dried bread crumbs
¼ tsp (1 mL) salt
½ tsp (2 mL) freshly ground black pepper
2 pork tenderloins (12 oz/375 g each)
2 tbsp (30 mL) olive oil 2 shallots, minced
1 large clove garlic, minced
2 sage leaves, chopped (or ½ tsp/2 mL dried)
4 oz (125 g) cream cheese, softened
½ cup (125 mL) fresh wild blueberries
rosemary jus (recipe follows)

Season bread crumbs with salt and pepper. Trim tenderloins of any fat and silverskin; roll in crumb mixture. In a large skillet, heat oil over medium-high heat and brown pork on all sides. Remove from pan, slice into 1-inch (2.5-cm) medallions and set aside. Return skillet to burner and sauté shallots and garlic 2 minutes.

Preheat oven to 350°F (180°C). In a bowl, combine shallots, garlic, sage and softened cheese; gently fold in blueberries. Place pork medallions on a baking sheet and press lightly; spread tops with cheese mixture. Bake until pork is barely pink in the centre and cheese is golden brown, about 15 minutes. Serve on a pool of Rosemary Jus.

Serves 4.

Rosemary Jus (supplied by authors)
1 oz (30 g) demi-glace powder mix
½ cup (125 mL) red wine
¾ cup (175 mL) water
1 sprig fresh rosemary

In a saucepan, whisk together the demi-glace powder, wine and water until blended. Add rosemary and bring to a boil over medium-high heat, stirring constantly. Reduce heat and simmer 3 minutes, stirring occasionally. Remove rosemary and serve warm.

Yields 1¼ cups (300 mL).

Grilled Salmon Tournedos with Blueberry, Fennel and Corn Salsa

L'Astral at Loews Le Concorde Hotel
Québec City, QC

The chefs at L'Astral recommend serving the salmon on a bed of wild rice accompanied with green asparagus and sautéed grape tomatoes. Remember to prepare the salsa well ahead of serving time.

1¼ lb (600 g) salmon fillet
olive oil
salt and freshly ground pepper
blueberry, fennel and corn salsa (recipe follows)

Slice the salmon fillet into four 1-inch (2.5-cm) slices. Roll salmon to form tournedos (round shapes) and secure each with a toothpick. Brush tournedos with olive oil, season with salt and pepper. Preheat grill to medium-high and grill salmon until opaque, about 4-5 minutes on each side. Serve immediately with blueberry, fennel and corn salsa.

Serves 4.

Blueberry, Fennel and Corn Salsa
This salsa can accompany many varieties of fish.
¼ cup (60 mL) chopped shallot
3 tbsp (45 mL) olive oil, portioned
2 tbsp (30 mL) white wine
1 cup (250 mL) pre-cooked corn kernels
½ cup (125 mL) diced sweet red pepper
1 fennel stalk, finely sliced
1 garlic clove, minced
12 small Shiitake mushroom caps
½ cup (125 mL) fresh wild blueberries
1½ tbsp (20 mL) fresh lemon juice
salt and freshly ground pepper
1-2 tsp (5-10 mL) blueberry vinegar (or red wine vinegar)

In a skillet, sweat the shallot in 1 tbsp (15 mL) olive oil until softened, about 5 minutes. Add the wine and reduce until the liquid has completely evaporated. Remove from heat and add the corn, red pepper, fennel, garlic and 1 tbsp (15 mL) olive oil. Return to heat, gently sauté a few minutes and then remove from heat.

In a small skillet, heat 1 tbsp (15 mL) olive oil and sauté the mushroom caps until lightly golden. Slice mushrooms in slivers. Transfer mushrooms and blueberries to salsa mixture. Stir in lemon juice and adjust seasoning with salt, pepper and vinegar to taste.

Blueberry Orange Compote with Lemonade Sauce and Cinnamon Ice Cream in a Crisp Cookie Cup, p.72

Desserts

Ah, this is what you've been waiting for! An endless array of tempting blueberry desserts—need we say more? For a light conclusion, try Blueberry Sorbet. But to really impress your dinner guests, serve the spectacular Blueberry Ballerina or decadent Blueberry and White Chocolate Victoria.

Blueberry Spice Chiffon Cake

Gowrie House Country Inn, Sydney Mines, NS

The innkeeper of Gowrie House tells us that this cake is equally delicious when made with fresh strawberries and decadent when made with fresh raspberries. We can't wait to try his suggestions!

2¼ cups (550 mL) cake flour
1½ cups (375 mL) granulated sugar
1 tbsp (15 mL) baking powder
1 tsp (5 mL) cinnamon
¾ tsp (4 mL) salt
6 eggs, separated
½ cup (125 mL) vegetable oil
¾ cup (175 mL) water
1½ tsp (7 mL) vanilla
¼ tsp (1 mL) cream of tartar
1 cup (250 mL) heavy cream (35% M.F.)
2 tbsp (30 mL) brown sugar
1 quart (1 L) fresh blueberries
2 cups (500 mL) heavy cream (35% M.F.) (2nd amount)
¼ cup (60 mL) granulated sugar (2nd amount)

Preheat oven to 325°F (180°C). Combine flour, 1 cup (250 mL) of the sugar, baking powder, cinnamon and salt in a large mixing bowl. Separate eggs. Combine yolks, oil, water and vanilla in a small bowl. In a large metal bowl, beat egg whites with cream of tartar at medium speed until soft peaks form. Gradually beat in remaining ½ cup (125 mL) of sugar, a spoonful at a time, beating at high speed until stiff peaks form.

Combine egg yolk mixture with flour mixture, beating just until smooth. Carefully fold egg whites into cake batter, in four additions. Pour into an ungreased 10-inch (25-cm) tube pan and bake 1 hour and 10 minutes. Remove from oven and cool on a wire rack. When completely cooled, loosen around edges and invert on rack.

To assemble, slice cake in half. Using the lower half of the cake, cut a 2-inch (5-cm) tunnel in centre of cake about ½ inch (1 cm) from the sides. Remove excess cake with a fork to form a tunnel. Whip 1 cup (250 mL) of heavy cream with brown sugar until stiff peaks form. Fold in blueberries, reserving ¼ cup (60 mL) for garnish. Fill tunnel and gently cover with upper half of cake. Whip remaining 2 cups (500 mL) of heavy cream with ¼ cup (60 mL) of sugar and decorate cake. Garnish with reserved berries.

Serves 12.

Blueberry Glacé Tart

Duncreigan Country Inn, Mabou, NS

Eleanor Mullendore of the Duncreigan Country Inn tells us that as a variation, this recipe can be prepared with fresh strawberries or raspberries in season.

Tart Pastry
1 cup (250 mL) all-purpose flour
⅓ cup (75 mL) pastry flour
1 tbsp (15 mL) granulated sugar
⅓ cup (75 mL) unsalted butter, chilled
2 tbsp (30 mL) vegetable shortening, chilled
3-4 tbsp (45-60 mL) ice water

Mix dry ingredients together in a bowl. Cut in butter and shortening with a pastry blender until mixture resembles coarse crumbs. Stir in cold water just until dough sticks together. Form into a smooth ball and wrap in plastic wrap; chill 30 minutes. Preheat oven to 425°F (220°C). Roll pastry to fit a 9-inch (23-cm) tart or pie plate and chill 15 minutes. Prick well and bake until golden, about 12-15 minutes. Remove from oven and cool.

Filling
3 cups (750 mL) fresh blueberries, divided
¾ cup (175 mL) granulated sugar
1 tbsp (15 mL) lime juice
½ cup (125 mL) cream cheese, softened
sweetened whipped cream, as garnish (optional)

Cook 1 cup (250 mL) of the blueberries with the sugar until thickened. Purée until smooth; add lime juice and cool. Stir 1½ cups (375 mL) of the remaining berries into sauce.

Spread cream cheese over cooled pastry shell. Top with berry mixture. Sprinkle remaining ½ cup (125 mL) berries over top and chill until set. Garnish with sweetened whipped cream.

Serves 6-8.

Blueberry Ballerina

Inn on the Cove and Spa, Saint John, NB

This spectacular dessert is easy to prepare and is a variation of the famous pavlova, which uses strawberries and kiwi fruit. The meringue is best made when the humidity is low.

Meringue
4-6 egg whites, at room temperature
pinch of cream of tartar
1 cup (250 mL) granulated sugar
1 tbsp (15 mL) cornstarch
pinch of salt
1 tsp (5 mL) vanilla
2 tsp (10 mL) cider vinegar
1 cup (250 mL) heavy cream (35% M.F.),
  whipped with 1 tbsp (15 mL) sugar
1½ cups (375 mL) fresh blueberries
blueberry coulis (recipe follows)

Preheat oven to 400°F (200°C). Beat egg whites and cream of tartar while gradually adding sugar. When all sugar is incorporated continue to beat until whites are very stiff. Fold in cornstarch and salt. Mix in vanilla and vinegar.

Cut two pieces of waxed paper to fit a large baking sheet. Thoroughly wet waxed paper sheets with cold water and place on baking sheet. Pile meringue in a circle with the sides slightly higher than the centre. Place in preheated 400°F (200°C) oven and immediately turn off heat. Leave in oven 1½ hours. Remove, let stand 10 minutes then separate from waxed paper and cool.

Place meringue on serving plate, fill with sweetened whipped cream and top with blueberries. Serve individual portions drizzled with blueberry coulis.

Serves 8-10.

Blueberry Coulis (supplied by authors)
2 cups (500 mL) fresh or frozen blueberries
½ cup (125 mL) granulated sugar, or to taste
¼ cup (60 mL) water
2 tsp (10 mL) cornstarch, dissolved in 1 tbsp
  (15 mL) cold water
2 tsp (10 mL) fresh lemon juice

In a heavy saucepan, bring blueberries, sugar and water to a boil, stirring occasionally, 5 minutes. Prepare cornstarch mixture and stir into pan. Add lemon juice and simmer for 2 minutes, stirring constantly. Strain sauce, then chill until cold. To serve, mound meringue with whipped cream, sprinkle with fresh berries and drizzle with blueberry sauce.

Blueberry Grunt

Mountain Gap Inn, Smiths Cove, NS

Blueberry Grunt is the homey kind of dessert we all shared around our grandmother's table. At Mountain Gap Inn, it is served warm with vanilla ice cream or whipped cream.

Sauce
2 cups (500 mL) fresh or frozen blueberries
¼-½ cup (50-125 mL) granulated sugar
⅓ cup (75 mL) water

Dumplings
1 cup (250 mL) all-purpose flour
2 tsp (10 mL) baking powder
1 tsp (5 mL) granulated sugar
¼ tsp (1 mL) salt
½ tbsp (7 mL) butter
½ tbsp (7 mL) shortening
⅓-½ cup (75-125 mL) milk
vanilla ice cream or whipped cream, as garnish

Wash and drain berries, combine with sugar and water and bring to a boil in a large saucepan. Reduce heat and simmer until berries are soft and sauce begins to thicken, about 5 minutes.

Whisk together flour, baking powder, sugar and salt. Cut in butter and shortening with a pastry blender. Stir in just enough milk to make a soft dough. Drop the batter by spoonfuls on top of the simmering berry sauce. Immediately cover saucepan and cook over medium heat without removing cover for 15-18 minutes. Serve warm with ice cream or whipped cream.

Serves 4-6.

Caramel Chocolate Crème with Warm Blueberry Sauce

Dufferin Inn and San Martello Dining Room
Saint John, NB

Margret and Axel Begner serve this decadent crème caramel topped with a warm blueberry sauce. The subtle addition of chocolate to the custard makes it a memorable dessert!

½ cup (125 mL) granulated sugar
1 tbsp (15 mL) water
1 cup (250 mL) milk
1 cup (250 mL) heavy cream (35% M.F.)
2 squares white chocolate
3 egg yolks
2 whole eggs
blueberry sauce (recipe follows)

Note: Caramel reaches a very high temperature. We suggest you use oven mitts to protect yourself from splattering when the milk and cream are added.

Heat sugar and water in a heavy saucepan over low heat, shaking the pan occasionally until the sugar is dissolved. Turn heat to high and boil, without stirring, until caramel is golden brown. Watch carefully so that it does not burn.

Remove from heat and cautiously stir in the milk and cream. Return to heat and bring almost to a boil; add chocolate and stir until melted.

Preheat oven to 350°F (180°C).

In a bowl, combine yolks and whole eggs. Stir a small amount of the hot mixture into the eggs, return eggs to hot mixture and whisk to combine. Pour into six custard cups.

Place custard cups in a water bath and bake in a preheated 350°F (180°C) oven 30-35 minutes or until a knife inserted in the centre comes out clean. Cool, then chill.

To serve, unmold on individual serving plates and top with warm blueberry sauce.

Serves 6.

Blueberry Sauce
1½ cups (375 mL) blueberries
1 cup (250 mL) red wine
4 tbsp (60 mL) granulated sugar
1 tbsp (15 mL) cornstarch
1 tsp (5 mL) vanilla

Cook blueberries, wine, sugar and cornstarch in a saucepan over medium heat until thick and bubbly. Remove from heat, stir in vanilla and keep warm.

Blueberry Apple Flan

Haddon Hall Inn, Chester, NS

The chef at Haddon Hall Inn suggests that you may, for convenience, prepare the filling a day in advance. He also advises baking the flan on a cookie sheet, to avoid having the fruit bubble over into your oven.

Butter Pastry (Pâte Brisée)
1¼ cups (300 mL) all-purpose flour
¼ tsp (1 mL) salt
½ cup (125 mL) unsalted butter, softened
3 tbsp (45 mL) ice water

Combine flour and salt in a medium-sized bowl. Cut in butter with a pastry blender until the mixture resembles coarse meal. Sprinkle with enough water to hold dough together. Form into a ball, wrap in plastic wrap and refrigerate 30 minutes.

Before removing from refrigerator, preheat oven to 400°F (200°C). Flatten dough between two sheets of plastic wrap to form a disc. Roll to fit a 10-inch (25-cm) flan pan. Prick pastry and bake for 15 minutes. Cool.

Filling
1¼ cups (300 mL) apple cider
1 scant cup (250 mL) granulated sugar
1¼ cups (300 mL) fresh blueberries
4 medium cooking apples, peeled and sliced

Heat cider and sugar until sugar dissolves, then boil 2 minutes. Add blueberries and sliced apples and return to a boil. Reduce heat and simmer until apples are tender, about 5 minutes. Transfer to a bowl, chill and reserve.

Remove fruit from bowl with a slotted spoon and arrange over flan pastry. Top with streusel mixture (below) and bake at 400°F (200°C) for 30-35 minutes, until topping has browned and filling is bubbling.

Serves 6-8.

Streusel Topping
½ cup (125 mL) flour
⅓ cup (75 mL) dark brown sugar
⅓ cup (75 mL) unsalted butter
½ cup (125 mL) pecans, coarsely chopped

Combine flour, brown sugar and butter. Add pecan pieces and sprinkle over prepared flan.

Blomidon Inn Blueberry Shortcake

Blomidon Inn, Wolfville, NS

"This is no ordinary shortcake," states Jim Laceby, owner of Blomidon Inn. Diners agree with the claim, making it one of the more popular desserts during berry season.

Shortcakes

¼ cup (60 mL) softened butter
3 tbsp (45 mL) granulated sugar
2 eggs
1 tbsp (15 mL) lemon zest
2 tbsp (30 mL) fresh lemon juice
½ cup light cream (10% M.F.)
2 cups (500 mL) all-purpose flour
1 tbsp (15 mL) baking powder
pinch of salt
blueberry sauce (recipe follows)
whipped cream, as garnish

Preheat oven to 375°F (190°C). Cream butter and sugar together in the bowl of a mixer, until light and fluffy. Beat in eggs, lemon zest, lemon juice and blend. Sift flour, baking powder and salt together and gradually stir into the egg mixture, being careful not to overmix. Turn shortcake out onto a floured surface, turn to coat other side and gently press to ¾-inch (2-cm) thickness. Cut shortcakes with a 3-inch (8-cm) cutter, and place on an ungreased cookie sheet 1½ inches (4 cm) apart. Bake for 15 minutes or until puffed and lightly browned on the bottom. Cool on wire racks.

To serve, split shortcake, spoon blueberry sauce onto the bottom half and cover with the top of the shortcake. Garnish with whipped cream.

Serves 6-8.

Blueberry Sauce

2 cups (500 mL) fresh blueberries
¾ cup (175 mL) granulated sugar
½ cup (125 mL) water
1 tbsp (15 mL) cornstarch

Combine blueberries, sugar and a little of the water in a heavy saucepan over medium heat; cook and stir until berries burst. Continue to cook until sauce begins to boil. Combine cornstarch and remaining water and whisk into sauce. Return to boil and cook until sauce thickens. Makes 1½ cups (375 mL) sauce.

Cold Blueberry Soufflé

La Perla, Dartmouth, NS

This is an impressive dessert that is easy to prepare in advance. At La Perla, it is presented in individual dishes decorated with a dollop of whipped cream and fresh mint leaves or spring flowers.

5 cups (1.25 L) blueberries, fresh or frozen
2 tbsp (30 mL) water
2 tbsp (30 mL) Grand Marnier liqueur
1½ envelopes gelatin
3 egg whites
½ cup (125 mL) granulated sugar
1½ cups (375 mL) heavy cream (35% M.F.), whipped

Prepare a 1½-qt (1.5-L) soufflé dish with a foil collar.

In a deep saucepan, cook blueberries and water over medium heat until berries have broken down and mixture has become a sauce. Remove from heat and stir in Grand Marnier. Keep warm.

In a small bowl, sprinkle gelatin over 3 tbsp (45 mL) of cold water and stir. Set aside for 5 minutes to dissolve, then stir into blueberry sauce.

Whisk egg whites and sugar until frothy and place in the top of a double boiler over hot (not boiling) water. Cook, whisking constantly, until thick and sugar is completely dissolved. Remove from heat and set double boiler insert in a bowl of ice.

Carefully fold blueberry mixture into egg whites. Fold in whipped cream and pour into the prepared soufflé dish. Refrigerate for 4 hours or until set.

To serve, remove foil collar and decorate as desired.

Serves 4.

Blueberry Orange Compote with Lemonade Sauce and Cinnamon Ice Cream in a Crisp Cookie Cup

The Inn at Bay Fortune, Bay Fortune, PEI

Chef Michael Smith has created a winner and a work of art. The flavours and textures of this delightful dessert are simply "sinful."

Compote
2 oranges
2 cups (500 mL) blueberries
2 tbsp (30 mL) Grand Marnier liqueur
¼ cup (60 mL) icing sugar, sifted

Zest (thinly grate rind), peel and section oranges, being careful to discard all pith. Combine zest, orange sections, blueberries, Grand Marnier and icing sugar in a bowl. Cover and reserve for ½ hour to allow flavours to blend.

Lemonade Sauce
⅓ cup (75 mL) granulated sugar
2 lemons, zest (thinly grated peel) and juice
⅓ cup (75 mL) water
2 medium apples, cored and chopped

Combine sugar, lemon zest, juice, water and apples in a small saucepan. Bring to a boil, stirring until sugar dissolves; reduce heat and simmer for 15 minutes. Purée in a blender until sauce is smooth and then strain through a fine-mesh strainer. Reserve and cool.

Crisp Cookie Cups
¼ cup (60 mL) butter
¼ cup (60 mL) corn syrup
2½ tbsp (40 mL) brown sugar
⅓ cup (75 mL) cake flour
½ cup (125 mL) ground walnuts

Preheat oven to 350°F (180°C). In a heavy saucepan, combine butter, corn syrup and sugar over medium heat; bring to a boil, stirring constantly. Remove from heat. Combine flour and ground nuts and add to sugar mixture, stirring to form a batter.

Drop spoonfuls of batter onto greased baking sheets about 4 inches (10 cm) apart. Bake for 6-8 minutes, until golden brown and bubbly. Remove from oven and let cool for 30 seconds or until edges easily lift with a spatula. Immediately drape hot cookie over inverted custard cups, gently pressing to the form. (If cookies become too brittle to shape, return to oven just until softened.) Cool on wire racks. May be made up to 48 hours in advance and stored in an airtight container.

Cinnamon Ice Cream
1 pint (500 mL) good-quality vanilla ice cream
1 tbsp (15 mL) cinnamon sugar

Stir cinnamon sugar into slightly softened ice cream. Return to freezer.

To serve: place crisp cookie cup on serving plate. Fill with a scoop of cinnamon ice cream, spoon compote around ice cream and drizzle with lemonade sauce.

Serves 6-8.

Blueberry and Rhubarb Crumble

Dalvay by the Sea, Dalvay, PEI

Executive chef Richard Kemp of Dalvay by the Sea serves this delicious fruit dessert hot, with frozen berry yoghurt.

Filling

2 tbsp (30 mL) butter
⅔ cup (150 mL) granulated sugar, or to taste
1½ tbsp (20 mL) lemon juice
1 lb (0.5 kg) rhubarb, chopped
1 cup (250 mL) blueberries
½ tsp (2 mL) cinnamon
½ tsp (2 mL) vanilla

Crumble

⅓ cup (75 mL) butter, softened
½ cup (125 mL) granulated sugar
½ cup (125 mL) all-purpose flour
½ cup (125 mL) ground almonds
⅓ cup (75 mL) rolled oats

In a saucepan combine butter, sugar and lemon juice; cook and stir over medium heat until lightly golden. Add rhubarb and increase heat to medium-high. Cook and stir until it starts to thicken, approximately 10 minutes. Add blueberries and cinnamon and cook for an additional 4 minutes. Remove from heat, stir in vanilla and cool.

Preheat oven to 425°F (220°C). Cream butter and sugar until smooth. Combine flour, almonds and oats; gradually rub into butter mixture until crumbly. Pour rhubarb-blueberry mixture into a greased two-quart (2-L) baking dish and sprinkle crumble mixture on top. Bake for 25-30 minutes, until top is browned. (May also be baked in 6 individual ramekins for 10-12 minutes.) Serve warm with frozen yoghurt or whipped cream.

Serves 6.

Wild Blueberry Posset

Acton's Grill and Café, Wolfville, NS

The chef at Acton's serves this refreshing dessert in a glass dish garnished with a few sprigs of fresh mint, whole fresh blueberries and some cookies on the side.

2 cups (500 mL) fresh wild blueberries, crushed
½ cup (125 mL) granulated sugar
2 cups (500 mL) heavy cream (35% M.F.), whipped
2 tbsp (30 mL) lemon juice
4 egg whites

Combine crushed blueberries with sugar, whipped cream and lemon juice. Set aside. Beat egg whites until stiff but not dry; carefully fold into blueberry and cream mixture. Spoon into individual dessert dishes and serve immediately.

Yields 8 servings.

Classic English Trifle

Garrison House Inn, Annapolis Royal, NS

Patrick Redgrave of the Garrison House Inn prepares his trifle using many seasonal fruits. We find that blueberries and bananas are a winning combination.

8-10 ladyfingers (or 1 sponge cake)
½ cup (125 mL) blueberry jam
¼ cup (60 mL) sherry
1½ cups (375 mL) sliced bananas
1½ cups (375 mL) fresh blueberries
custard (recipe follows)
½ cup (125 mL) heavy cream (35% M.F.)
½ tsp (2 mL) vanilla
¼ cup (60 mL) sliced almonds

Split ladyfingers or cake and spread with thick layer of jam. Arrange pieces over the bottom of a shallow, clear glass bowl. Sprinkle with sherry. Arrange fruit on cake.

Prepare custard and while still warm pour over trifle. Let stand at room temperature until cool, then refrigerate.

To serve, whip cream until stiff and add vanilla. Spread over custard and top with almonds.

Serves 6-8.

Custard (supplied by authors)
¼ cup (60 mL) granulated sugar
3 tbsp (45 mL) all-purpose flour
3 egg yolks, beaten
2 cups (500 mL) milk
2 tsp (10 mL) lemon zest (thinly grated peel)
1 tsp (5 mL) vanilla

In a heavy saucepan, combine sugar, flour, egg yolks, milk and lemon zest. Cook, stirring over medium heat until mixture is thick and begins to boil. Remove from heat, add vanilla and cover with waxed paper.

Easy Blueberry Crème Brulée

Quaco Inn, St. Martins, NB

If you are looking for a quick and easy dessert recipe, look no further. This dessert is beautiful in appearance and oh, so tasty!

1 pint (500 mL) fresh blueberries
⅔ cup (150 mL) low-fat sour cream
½ cup (125 mL) plain yoghurt
⅓ cup (75 mL) brown sugar
mint leaves, as garnish

Divide blueberries among 6 heat-proof ramekins.

Combine sour cream and yoghurt and spread over blueberries, being careful to cover completely. Sprinkle brown sugar over sour cream and broil 3 inches (8 cm) from element until sugar caramelizes, approximately 3-5 minutes. Watch carefully, as topping can easily burn.

Serve immediately, garnished with mint leaves.

Serves 6.

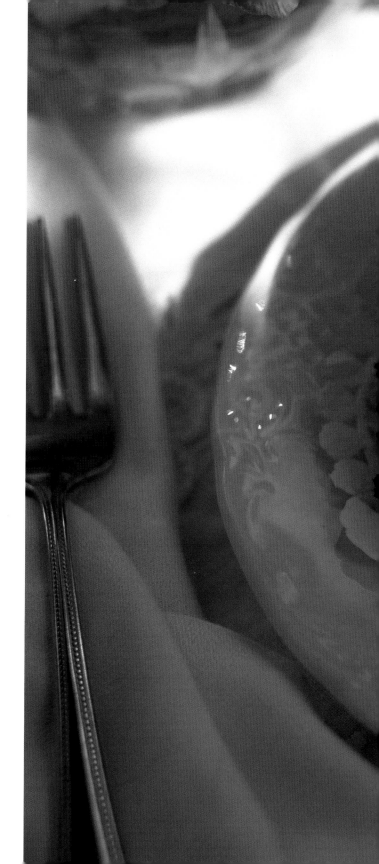

Ingonish Blueberry Flan

Keltic Lodge, Ingonish, NS

The chefs at Keltic Lodge use fresh local blueberries in this variation of a traditional flan. Serve it warm, plain or with a dollop of fresh whipped cream.

1 single pie crust (recipe follows)
½ cup (125 mL) milk
½ cup (125 mL) plain yoghurt
¾ cup (175 mL) granulated sugar
4 eggs, beaten
1½ tsp (7 mL) vanilla
3 cups (750 mL) fresh blueberries

Preheat oven to 375°F (190°C). Prepare pastry and arrange in a 9-inch (23-cm) diameter, ¾-inch (2-cm) deep, loose-bottomed flan or pie pan. Prick the crust with a fork and bake for 12 minutes.

In a saucepan, bring milk, yoghurt and sugar to a boil, stirring constantly. Stir small amount of hot mixture into eggs, return to hot mixture and cook until thickened, stirring constantly. Remove from heat and stir in vanilla.

Add blueberries to prepared pastry shell and pour custard over them. Bake for 25 minutes.

Serve warm.

Single Shell Pastry

1 cup (250 mL) all-purpose flour
¼ tsp (1 mL) salt
½ cup (125 mL) shortening
2-3 tbsp (30-45 mL) cold water

Combine flour and salt in mixing bowl. Cut shortening into flour with pastry blender until mixture is size of large peas. Do not overmix. Sprinkle cold water over mixture and blend with a fork until absorbed. Form into a ball and roll out on a floured surface.

Yields enough pastry for single shell.

Blueberry Grand Marnier Flan

Falcourt Inn, Nictaux, NS

Berry season is short, so plan to prepare this sumptuous dessert at least once during harvest time

Pastry

1 cup + 1 tbsp (265 mL) all-purpose flour
¼ cup (60 mL) granulated sugar
dash of salt
¾ tsp (4 mL) lemon zest (thinly grated peel)
¼ cup (60 mL) butter, softened
2 egg yolks, beaten

Preheat oven to 350°F (180°C). Blend together the flour, sugar, salt and zest. Cut in butter and bind together with egg yolks. Press into the bottom and up the sides of a greased 10-inch (25-cm) flan pan. Bake for 10 minutes. Cool.

Filling

¾ cup (175 mL) granulated sugar
¼ cup (60 mL) cornstarch
1½ cups (375 mL) milk
2 eggs
1 tbsp (15 mL) butter
1 tsp (5 mL) vanilla
1½ tbsp (20 mL) Grand Marnier liqueur
3 cups (750 mL) fresh blueberries
½ cup (125 mL) granulated sugar (2nd amount)
3 tbsp (45 mL) apricot jam

Preheat oven to 350°F (180°C). In the top half of a double boiler over simmering water, combine sugar and cornstarch. Whisk in milk and bring to a boil, stirring constantly. In a small bowl, beat eggs, stir in a little of the hot milk mixture, then return to the double boiler and cook until thick and smooth. Remove from heat and stir in butter, vanilla and Grand Marnier. Pour into prepared flan pastry.

Mix together blueberries and sugar and sprinkle evenly over custard. Bake for 30-35 minutes, or until berries are cooked. Melt apricot jam with 1 tsp (5 mL) water and brush over berries. Serve chilled with whipped cream for a garnish, if desired.

Blueberry Sorbet

Little Inn of Bayfield, Bayfield, ON

For best results, prepare the sorbet a day ahead. When blueberries aren't available, substitute another favourite berry.

1 cup (250 mL) granulated sugar
½ cup (125 mL) freshly-squeezed lemon juice
6 cups (1.5 L) fresh blueberries

In a saucepan, dissolve the sugar in lemon juice over medium heat. Add blueberries and cook over low heat, stirring occasionally until berries are soft. Remove from heat and cool slightly. In a blender, purée mixture until smooth. Chill the mixture for four hours; do not let it freeze.

When very cold, pour the mixture into an ice cream machine and freeze following manufacturer's directions.

Yields 6 cups (1.5 L).

Blueberry Charlotte

Amherst Shore Country Inn, Lorneville, NS

Blueberries are Nova Scotia's official berry, and the Amherst Shore Country Inn serves a delightful assortment of blueberry dishes. This "Charlotte" is light and airy—the perfect dessert to end a perfect meal.

3 eggs
½ tsp (2 mL) cream of tartar
⅓ cup (75 mL) ice water
¾ cup (175 mL) granulated sugar
1 tsp (5 mL) almond extract
½ cup (175 mL) all-purpose flour
½ tsp (2 mL) baking powder
3 tbsp (45 mL) crème de cassis liqueur
1 cup (250 mL) blueberry conserve
  (see page 27)
crème anglaise (recipe follows)

Preheat oven to 350°F (180°C). Grease two 8-inch (20-cm) cake pans and line with waxed paper. Lightly grease and flour paper.

Separate eggs. Using an electric mixer, beat egg whites with cream of tartar until stiff. Set aside. In a separate bowl, beat yolks until pale and thick. Add ice water and continue to beat for another 3-4 minutes. Add sugar and almond extract, beating for an additional 4 minutes. Using a rubber spatula, fold in flour and baking powder. Gently fold in egg whites. Divide batter between pans and bake until golden brown and a tester comes out clean, approximately 20-25 minutes. Loosen edges, turn cakes out onto a rack and remove waxed paper. Cool completely.

To assemble, split each cake in half. Place one bottom piece on a plate. Sprinkle with 1 tbsp (15 mL) crème de cassis and spread with ⅓ cup (75 mL) blueberry conserve. Repeat twice more and cover with top of second cake. Completely wrap with plastic wrap and refrigerate.

Slice in wedges and serve on a bed of crème anglaise.

Serves 8.

Crème Anglaise
¾ cup (175 mL) heavy cream (35% M.F.)
¾ cup (175 mL) whole milk (3.25% M.F.)
3 egg yolks
3 tbsp (45 mL) icing sugar

Heat, but do not boil, the cream and milk in the top of a double boiler over hot water. Whisk together yolks and icing sugar. Stir a small amount of the hot mixture into the yolks. Return yolks to hot mixture and cook gently until mixture lightly coats the back of a spoon. Remove from heat, cover top of sauce with plastic wrap and chill.

Yields 1½ cups (375 mL).

Blueberry and Orange Blossom Cheesecake

All Seasons Café, Nelson, BC

Chef Adam Druitt of All Seasons Café bakes his cheesecake using the *bain-marie*, or water bath, method. This allows him to spoon the dessert into pre-baked phyllo cups and decorate his plate in a variety of ways. Remember to thaw frozen phyllo pastry in the refrigerator overnight before using.

4 sheets phyllo pastry
½ cup (125 mL) butter, melted
12 oz (375 g) cream cheese, softened
½ cup (125 mL) granulated sugar
2 tbsp (30 mL) heavy cream (35% M.F.)
4 tbsp (60 mL) pure maple syrup
1 tbsp (15 mL) orange blossom water*
2 whole eggs
1 egg yolk
1 cup (250 mL) wild blueberries
Additional blueberries, maple syrup and mint
    leaves, as garnish (optional)

Thaw phyllo pastry in the refrigerator overnight. Preheat oven to 375°F (190°C). Brush 1 sheet of phyllo pastry with melted butter. Cover with a second sheet and brush with butter. Repeat with remaining sheets. Grease 6 muffin tins with rest of butter. Cut pastry into 4-inch (10-cm) squares and gently fit into muffin pans. Bake tart shells 10 minutes or until golden brown. Cool in pan, then remove to wire rack and reserve.

Preheat oven to 350°F (180°C). In a mixer using medium speed, combine cream cheese, sugar, cream and maple syrup. Stir in orange blossom water and incorporate eggs and yolk one at a time, beating until well blended. Using a rubber spatula, gently fold in berries. Turn batter into an ungreased 1-quart (1-L) ovenproof bowl. Set bowl in a shallow pan; pour hot water around the bowl, 2 inches (5 cm) deep. Bake until dessert is set, 50-60 minutes (longer for frozen berries). Remove from water bath, cool to room temperature and chill in refrigerator.

To serve, spoon cheesecake into phyllo cups. Garnish, if desired, with additional blueberries, a drizzle of maple syrup and fresh mint leaves.

Serves 6.

*Orange blossom water is a flavouring distilled from the blossoms of Seville oranges. It is available in specialty food stores.

Blueberry Flan

Amherst Shore Country Inn, Lorneville, NS

Donna Laceby at the Amherst Shore Country Inn suggests adding a little tapioca to absorb some of the juices if you are using frozen blueberries. For a lighter dessert, use low-fat sour cream and omit the whipped cream garnish.

Crust

1½ cups (375 mL) all-purpose flour
½ cup (125 mL) granulated sugar
1½ tsp (7 mL) baking powder
½ cup (125 mL) butter, softened
1 egg
½ tsp (2 mL) almond extract

Filling

5 cups (1.25 L) fresh or frozen unthawed
   blueberries
2 tbsp (30 mL) orange liqueur
1 tsp (5 mL) lemon zest (thinly grated rind)
4 tsp (20 mL) minute tapioca, if using frozen
   berries

Topping

2 cups (500 mL) sour cream
½ cup (125 mL) granulated sugar
2 egg yolks
½ tsp (2 mL) almond extract
⅔ cup (150 mL) heavy cream (35% M.F.),
   whipped, as garnish

Preheat oven to 350°F (180°C). To prepare crust, blend flour, sugar, baking powder and butter in a mixing bowl. Add egg and almond extract and blend. Pat dough over the base of a greased 10½-inch (27-cm) springform pan.

Mix together blueberries, liqueur, lemon zest and minute tapioca, if using frozen berries. Spoon onto crust.

Combine topping ingredients and mix well. Spoon evenly over blueberries in crust. Bake at 350°F (180°C) for 1¼ hours or until crust is golden and berries are tender. Let cool, then refrigerate. Just before serving, top generously with whipped cream.

Serves 10-12.

Fresh Blueberry and White Chocolate Victoria

Vineland Estates Winery Restaurant, Vineland, ON

The chef tells us that the "Victoria" is a classic Canadian dessert whose ancestor, a fruit-laden picnic cake known as the Victoria Sandwich, was enjoyed by the British gentry on the lawns of British Columbia's capital a century ago. Today the dessert has more humble applications and has evolved into a small tart. Rest assured that it is still delicious, rich and fruity. Feel free to substitute other fresh seasonal fruit for the blueberries.

1¼ cups (300 mL) all-purpose flour
¼ cup (50 mL) granulated sugar
pinch of salt
5 tbsp (75 mL) butter, diced
1 egg
1½-2 cups (375-500 mL) fresh blueberries
white chocolate ganache (recipe follows)

Sift flour into a bowl, add sugar and salt, and stir to combine. Rub butter into flour mixture with your fingers until it resembles fine crumbs. Make a well in centre of bowl. Lightly beat egg and pour into the well. Combine until dough comes together and can be formed into a ball. Do not overwork the dough. Wrap in plastic wrap and let rest 20 minutes.

Roll out dough on a floured surface to ⅛-inch (3-mm) thickness. Cut appropriate shapes for your tartlet molds. Line molds with dough, trim edges and prick bottom with a fork. Place another mold inside and press gently to secure. (This process is called "blind baking" and keeps the crust from shrinking.) Bake in preheated 350°F (180°C) oven for 10 minutes, remove top mold and bake a further 5-10 minutes or until tarts are lightly browned. Unmold and cool on wire rack.

To assemble: place a heap of blueberries in each tart and pour the warm chocolate ganache over top. Allow to sit in a cool place, but do not chill. Serve at room temperature. Makes 6-12 tarts depending upon size of tart molds.

Serves 4-6.

White Chocolate Ganache
Make this topping with the best-quality chocolate available, such as Lindt or Callebaut.
½ cup (125 mL) heavy cream (35% M.F.)
1 cup (250 mL) good-quality white baking
   chocolate

Chop chocolate and place in a bowl. In a small saucepan, bring cream to a boil. Immediately pour over chocolate and stir until smooth.

Warm Fruit Compote

Pines Resort, Digby, NS

Chefs at the Pines serve this delightful blend of
fresh fruits in a baked phyllo shell or as a filling
for dessert crèpes. We also tried it spooned over
frozen yoghurt or vanilla ice cream.

¾ cup (175 mL) fresh cranberries
¾ cup (175 mL) pears, peeled and diced
¾ cup (175 mL) apples, peeled and diced
¼ cup (60 mL) fresh blueberries
¼ cup (60 mL) brown sugar
⅛ tsp (0.5 mL) cloves
⅛ tsp (0.5 mL) allspice
¼ tsp (1 mL) cinnamon
whipped cream, as garnish

Combine all ingredients in a large saucepan and
cook slowly for 5-7 minutes, stirring
occasionally. Serve in a phyllo shell with a dollop
of whipped cream or as a basis for other
desserts.

Serves 4-6.

Blueberry, Mango and Hazelnut Cobbler

Old House Restaurant, Courtenay, BC

Easy to prepare and even easier to consume, this cobbler is delicious warm or at room temperature and served with or without vanilla ice cream. Feel free to substitute pears, peaches, apples or raspberries for the mango, and walnuts or pecans for the hazelnuts.

⅔ cup (150 mL) all-purpose flour
⅔ cup (150 mL) brown sugar
½ cup (125 mL) butter, softened
3 cups (750 mL) peeled mango, cut in ½-inch (1-cm) cubes
2 cups (500 mL) blueberries (fresh or frozen)
1 cup (250 mL) chopped hazelnuts
3 tbsp (45 mL) cornstarch

In a bowl, mix together the flour and sugar. Add butter and blend with fingertips until the consistency of oatmeal; reserve.

In a 2-qt (2-L) ovenproof dish, combine mango, blueberries and hazelnuts. Sprinkle with cornstarch and stir to mix. Distribute topping mixture over fruit and bake in preheated 375°F (190°C) oven 30-40 minutes until lightly browned and bubbly around the edges. Note: it takes slightly longer to bake with frozen fruit.

Serve warm or at room temperature with vanilla ice cream or by itself.

Serves 6.

Blueberry Financiers

Edgewater Manor Restaurant, Stoney Creek, ON

Cookie-sized, but with the consistency of a light sponge cake, these delightful little morsels are French in origin. Financiers and madeleines are close relatives, the only difference being the type of pan used. Though both desserts are commonly flavoured with lemon, the chefs at the Edgewater Manor Restaurant prefer small wild blueberries. The results are delectable.

¾ cup (175 mL) icing sugar, sifted
⅓ cup (75 mL) cake flour
1¼ cup (300 mL) finely ground almonds
¼ cup (60 mL) extra-fine sugar
6 egg whites
½ cup (125 mL) butter, melted
1 cup (250 mL) wild blueberries
⅓ cup (75 mL) blueberry jam

In a large bowl, mix together icing sugar, flour, almonds and sugar. Beat egg whites until frothy and stir into flour mixture. Stir butter into mixture and fold in blueberries. Spoon or pipe batter into lightly-greased financier molds, filling three-quarters full. Bake in preheated 350°F (180°C) oven until lightly puffed and golden, about 12-15 minutes. Unmold immediately and cool on wire racks.

In a small saucepan, heat jam until melted. With a pastry brush, coat the molded side of each financier and return to rack to cool.

Makes 3 dozen.

Index

Photo Credits

Cover: All photos by Janet Kimber

Formac Publishing: (Meghan Collins: pages 1, 3, 5, 21, 22, 26, 31, 32, 36, 47, 48-49, 57, 80, 90, 92, 96; Robert MacGregor: pages 14-15, 24, 27, 33, 53, 72, 88); Steven Isleifson: pages 16, 28-29, 38-39, 41, 42, 45, 54-55, 61, 63, 64, 67, 68, 71, 73, 75, 76, 78-79, 85, 91; Janet Kimber: pages 17, 18, 23, 25, 30, 35, 37, 51, 52, 83, 87, 93; Nova Scotia Fisheries and Agriculture: pages 4, 8, 9 (top), 10, 11, 12, 13; Wild Blueberry Producers Association of Nova Scotia: pages 6, 7, 9 (bottom); Keith Vaughan: page 58

Food styling by James MacDougall